A CATALOGUE OF RISK

A CATALOGUE OF RISK

Alisha
Mascarenhas

Wendy's Subway

Sometimes you are privileged with a glimpse of the other world, when the light shines up from the west as the sun sets and dazzles something wet. The world is just water and light, a slide show through which your spirit guides.

—Fanny Howe, *Night Philosophy*

CONTENTS

	INTRODUCTION	9
	A NOTE ON TRANSLATION	11
	UNDERCURRENTS	13
PART I	BEAUTY	17
	BEWILDERMENT	23
	GLARING	25
	DISRUPTION	27
	INTIMATE PROPHECY	29
	REST	31
PART II	THE DISSOLUTION OF SELF	35
	ASSIDUITY	39
	BEING PERCEIVED	43
	TIME	45
	TOTALITY	49
	IN SUSPENSE	53
	SHAME	57
	DEPENDENCY	61
	HOPE NO MORE	67
	NOT DYING	70
PART III	PASSION	75
	FIDELITY	81
	BREAKING UP	87
	REGRET	89
	ZERO RISK	91

PART IV	SPEECH	95
	SPEECH (REPRISE)	97
	NOT KNOWING	99
	FAILURE	101
	FACILITY	103
PART V	SWEET DESCENT	107
	A COLD, DARK LAKE	111
	CONTRADICTION	115
	FAITH	117
	VOID	119
	LONGING	123
	MORTAL PROVIDENCE	125
	ENDNOTES	129

INTRODUCTION

I began writing these poems searching for a means to get closer to the risks inherent in daily life and intimacy. In *Éloge du risque (In Praise of Risk)*, philosopher and psychoanalyst Anne Dufourmantelle *(1964 - 2017) examines* the question of risk as it emerges among her various patients' lives. In attending to the specificity of an individual's historic conditions, Dufourmantelle's interpretation of their experiences exceeds individual diagnosis and opens toward the communal. Like this, each case study is fractal. As I read these experiences, I brought them into conversation with my own negotiations of risk: how to stay with the mysterious, terrifying, glorious indeterminacy of being alive.

    Risk became a guiding principle in my living by way of the contemplative space Dufourmantelle's book provides. I wanted to use writing as a method to participate in risk as it was alive for me in that moment; to slow things down in order to feel more; to suspend the immediacy of habitual reactions and linger in the choice to take a risk, or not, or not yet.

    Rather than adopt Dufourmantelle's "praise" of risk, I began to track, asking, *What, in this instance of experience, is at risk?* and writing through that experience. The title of each poem can, as such, be read as if preceded by the phrase, "At the risk of . . ."

    As time passes, I variously pursue and let rest the hidden logics of these poems, remaining curious while respecting their opacity. Meaning is always multiple, and I invite you, reader, to enter the risk of making your own.

A NOTE ON TRANSLATION

I initially read Dufourmantelle's work in its English translation by Steven Miller. Upon locating a copy of the original French text, I alternated between the two, and my reading of the original and its translation mingled. I eventually began to experiment with making my own translations of the French. I re-translated to get closer, deeper inside Dufourmantelle's book and what it held for me; to handle the text as material I could work with. Being inside a phrase mid-translation became another way to inhabit the liminal realm that holds the question of risk itself.

      The two texts (original and translation) became increasingly atmospheric as their questions hovered over and integrated into my thinking and being in a durational, continuous way. Most of these poems are introduced by direct excerpts from Dufourmantelle's original and its translation, whether my own or Miller's. Language from Dufourmantelle's book has also soaked into the poems, themselves receptive, porous things.

Dans toute écriture [. . .] il y a un texte sous-jacent à ce que l'on veut conduire en ligne de tête. [. . .] Ce sous-texte que l'inconscient arme comme il arme nos rêves, nos lapsus, nos actes manqués [. . .], là précisément se trouve à se risquer, vraiment, le désir.

In all writing . . . there is a text subjacent to that which we set out to write. This subtext that the unconscious arms as it arms our dreams, our slips of the tongue . . . precisely there, truly, desire is risked.

UNDERCURRENTS

All that we say to one another elapses time, runs through it
as an undercurrent, rippling with its own force, its own
knowing velocity. Each utterance from shore to shore a risk,
when beneath each line understood, there's always another.

We risk one another's interpretation of a tremble,
a hesitation at the level of the breath, the threat of a
darkening obscurity that swallows all subtlety.

I love not to know the totality of what I write to you
meaning comes of its own accord
incidentally, I will expose what I don't yet know myself
I'll be mistaken, misread & misunderstood
I'll hold your face in my hands
bite your lip to feel your pulse slow.

All of this tenuous, held in the faith of some subliminal
understanding: it's bodily, energetic, preceding the word.

Each line a transmission, and still
with the imperfect so hot in us
repeatedly we falter
fallible, retreating to shadowy pools
or the shade of dry & tangled brush.

I seek you out. Sit next to you in the shade to cool your
cheek with my hand, let it rest on the solid, living earth.

PART I

La beauté élève, bouleverse. Elle nous fixe là, dans ce qui ne nous appartient pas. Loin d'en être le sujet, celui qui l'éprouve en devient en quelque sorte la chose, pas au sens de l'objet mais d'un effet de résonance qui défait toute idée même d'appartenance ou de subjectivité.

Beauty elevates, overwhelms. It fixes us to the spot, in something that is not our own. Far from being the subject of beauty, one who experiences it in some sense becomes its thing—not an object so much as an effect of resonance that undoes the very idea of belonging or subjectivity.

BEAUTY

Examination is first attention.

Turning a corner toward the perfect light, sweet bloom, unplanned for pleasure, to risk being affected, being touched, losing touch, being called forth, the pleasure/ dread, Venusian nectar of attraction.

> What allows the perceptive faculties to open to beauty, to perceive it at all?

The perverse manifests in objectification: a function of force. I'm hungry for the light now, wanting it solid, immutable, a fixing down of something ephemeral, impermanent under the law of change.

*On entre dans la beauté comme dans
un cloître, lorsque la mesure se
répète et pourtant diffère; ce qui
s'élève alors [. . .] c'est
l'esprit qui opère en secret.*

*One enters beauty as into a
cloister, where its measure repeats,
yet differs; what arises, then . . .
is the spirit at work in secret.*

WITH KATHERINE BRADFORD'S PAINTING,
View Across Green (2017)

Deep enclosure being swallowed up by green, let rest
winter for the coming green, shimmer is beckoning a
dilation of the senses, endless depths of green

How pure and alive, quick snake in the water, ripple in
the glow, all entangled in green. How it holds you, makes
you whole & glowing in the gully. Wet depths of the
canyon, being feminine and alive in the perfect intelligence
of a colour, in the shadow of the moon, the slick cord of
the river

Entering time the way you enter a pool shining with weeds.
Being submerged. At the risk of becoming a part of what
you love, being deliberate in the dip or the dive, becoming
water is what you are; forgetting is another way to remember

I'm buckled into the consistency of the body   the
weather is electric   with summer rain   the syllables of
the afternoon align, reconciled to chance. I come back
with unwavering devotion, my love an immaterial fabric,
pliant generosity.   A tear in the   fabric   makes   it
wider,   just a slit in the cloth releases the   tension
makes   a   new   harmony   of the   surface;
ecstatic negative. *The true appears more true if
the real is deformed.*

It's just beginning: the will of travel, tenuous agency,
private repose in the chaos of midday. I am wandering
loose in the unknown: thirsty, particulate. Underslept
in the heat, I follow the feminine glint of light on a
necklace. The arches of my thinking are constrained by
this solitary discernment. There are deep reserves of
strength in me, still I tire quickly: by the sun, indecision,
too little nourishment of one kind or another. The play
of fact, function, how to float.

Days slip past, I let them. The beautiful surfaces of risk are presented daily: every instance of choice, the curve of the mistake, the turn that's made to adjust. What I need most is a room to come back to. I search out any stillness to learn the simple urgency of my desire. Time escapes me. I want to speak of more than doubt and uncertainty, but the unknown inhabits me like a ghost. I need sleep and some steady source to draw from.

Le risque, c'est de [. . .] perdre contrôle. Souffrir là où l'on croyait être tranquilles habitants de notre espace psychique, parce que nous préférons souvent à l'inconnu la connaissance de notre douleur.

Risk is . . . losing control. To suffer within what we believed to be a quiet existence in our psychic space, because we so often prefer the knowledge of our pain over the unknown.

BEWILDERMENT
after Fanny Howe

Weeping breaks the edge of September. Tall grasses moved by the wind in the yard of the blue house. Roses. Hard pears ripen on the tree and the cat rests on the tiles. She is gazing out the window. Floods of feeling come and go, indecipherable grief, this madness of waking each day in confusion. Time cruelly passing: minutes, hours, weeks, storms, visitors. Light slants away from you.

Bewilderment [is] a way of entering the day as much as the work.

I shut my eyes against the day but there is no retreat. This is a despair to live with, like the day I took the train to meet you, the whole ride wanting to die. It's so ordinary. You waited for me under the fountain outside the theatre and you lit my cigarette and showed me paintings of the sky. We sat in the cool, dark cinema and walked through the park and the moon rose over the city as we made our way to the cafe, holding hands and glancing back at each other, and the wind kicked up like it's doing now, and the roses are bright as ever and my mind is struck with doom and shifting shadows, how they rustle and flicker with the wind.

We are rushing *backwards and forwards within an irreconcilable set of imperatives.*

It's about the underside, but not only. The image behind the image. Life continues. The shadow is not the thing of life that cast it: this duality that holds our reality together. What's wrong comes underneath what's right.

*Risquer l'éblouissement
est dangereux parce que dans
ce trop de lumière ou de
vérité, il y a la possibilité
d'aveuglement définitif,
total, en la vie dans une
pénombre [. . .] . Mais
là est aussi l'apparition de
la joie.*

*Risking glare is dangerous
because in the too much
of light or truth resides
the possibility of permanent,
total blindness, life in
a penumbra . . . . But there,
too, is the apparition
of joy.*

GLARING

The glare of the day has put me on edge—
I'm on a downward track with this thinking
but I can't ignore the rattle

Every day shirking some violence, aggression,
ambivalent to escape, still seeking refuge
a little peace from the abrasive public

Constant alarm, eruptive hurt; impossible to be
excused, protected, apart: we hold the gravity
of these conditions in our bodies

Bitterness feeds bitterness & I'm looking out for the
long arc of truth, basic good. Every day I'm training my
defenses not to harden against this pain. I'm on a
downward track with this thinking. I can't ignore the rattle.

DISRUPTION

Morning between storms, an intellectual calm
is disrupted by some emergent stress, a kind of
heat, electric humidity: internal, environmental, both

I'm tracking indications of agitation versus ease
to go toward the latter, let loose the anticipatory
grip. When things get too mental I rest my head on something
solid, or go to water wherever I can get it

A revelatory light comes toward me: I blink, reset
the focus, its indistinct shimmering

I'm at a loss   for language
I'm running   past the flowers
I'm vaporous   in the bath
the sun emitting its hot, terrible light

Ce qui déroute la névrose, le « toujours déjà su », le « déjà connu », c'est la possibilité en nous de s'ouvrir à l'inédit, à un temps différent.

What derails neurosis, the "always already known," the "already understood" is the possibility within us of opening to the unprecedented, to a different time.

INTIMATE PROPHECY

After another spring night's rain, I am taking my coffee with cut tulips. The light at 8 am is silvery through the clouds. The resting state of illness has been good. I want life again, to choose it. I am tempering the rush, to stop striving.

Lightly we lay down preparation. Loosen the expectation. In a silent moment, I was permitted access to a possibility horizon. The performance of bondage that could set us free. The merge to let us float apart, still fastened by a long & flexible rope. I seek the routine that drops me into centre and the chance to sever automated inclinations, to split from the paths of habit, a rupture with the familiar. Contained derailment holds the risk.

I imagine being loved with all of this fear. All of this need, mutable emotion, pathetic lethargy. I imagine to not evolve beyond what limits me. To inhabit it.

No more striving. Imagine living as if it were already so. It is already so. The season is so good, come what may. I am, as Laura wrote on her birthday, *life loving to live living through me*. I have rested and I am coming to be with you, life, and it is glorious.

Yes, I'm resting in the spring light. Yes, I measure my effort by the rod of my desire & capacity. There is space & a bright wind in my chest. An inner smile. My tongue is relaxed & I feel a hunger within me. I'm alive. My gaze is curious and appreciative. I am determined to keep my fear from restricting the heart of any other. I close my eyes, relax my breath and a kind of serenity arises: I let it flood me.

REST
with Maren Karlson's pastel series
Angels 1-12

Form rises out of the darkness, wears with time. Angels celebrate the light of equinox. The green vinyl turns, shimmers with the season. Opal, onyx, raven's beak at dawn. Pitch, pitch the instrument through the channel to infinity. Spring glow empties the horizon.

How whole this body feels, how replenished. How long I've waited to feel supple, fluent, the edges totally softened. The future spills out before me like a continuous horizon, lapping. I will learn to act as if time is infinite before me. I'll force nothing, even as I secretly rush ahead. Where is my coat. I imagine stepping out: ocean come to me.

PART II

The Self is the ear of the ear,
The eye of the eye, the mind of the mind,
The word of words, and the life of life.
Rising above the senses and the mind
And renouncing separate existence,
The wise realizes the deathless Self.

    —The Kena Upanishad
    केनोपनिषद्

THE DISSOLUTION OF SELF

Always the hum of the mind
that extends toward relation
insistent, instinctive
the way that longing
is a sign of life:
do not punish it

This searching is in your nature
so what innocent satisfaction
in this perpetual thirst
to claim the lack
by naming it as such
like a spell, whereas
to withhold the word
recoil the attraction
is certain measure for stagnation

Yet the opposite must also be true
to remain silent and guard the force of the word in the body
effusive thought finds other channels

Desire lines open up
infinite options
exceed the intellect
the knower and the known
which cannot be separated
it's inherent
the light in the sky
is the light in your eyes

both familiar & mysterious
the good in you will always turn toward the good

You're crowned with sunbeams. Simplicity splinters at
daybreak and your pain lights up my world. You're down
by the water gazing out. I'm in advance of myself with
a tense and delicious secret. It is mine to hold and expose
as I choose: fan the flame, test the light, how it flickers.

The self becomes the self. Sleep overtakes me.
Valerian, water, plenitude. I'm full of fear, stupid with
misunderstanding. I've lost all my discipline and am
restless as an infant. I'm hungry for devotion. I'm high
on the genius of your endless multiplicities, come to me.
Your palms are open to the silence that follows the storm.

Imprecisely I move in and out of materiality—cosmos
blooming from the sidewalk. I'm infinite just like you,
breathing underwater, dreaming into the beyond from the
visual plane.

I'm standing still. I'm looking out from the dock in
my mind to the universal sunrise. I forgot how good it is
to feel. Innocent divinity is your true essence, love is
streaming out from my eyes, my forehead, I'm a fountain
for you.

*C'est tout le corps qui est érotique,
qui vibre, ressent et pense, qui
aime et se désespère, qui attend,
qui souffre et éprouve le plaisir
intense, infini d'être enveloppé.*

*It's the whole body that is
erotic, that vibrates,
feels and thinks, that loves
and despairs, that waits,
that suffers and feels the
intense, infinite pleasure
of being enveloped.*

ASSIDUITY

The determined light turns toward you
the sum of its effort
in the ripening apricot
the generous shade
passes, changes, closes in
obsession travels through the
nervous system, root system
neural pathways
the wild labours of its fruition
in the sun, the effort of acceptance
transpires in murmurs
a glance hardens to a stare, a pit, a stone
focused to the bone

The decision dares to overcome the problem
it's spiritual, practical, emotional
the plunging desire to fuck
irrevocable border of want

It refuses passivity, will not
be sublimated into a form other
than this noxious work
this dedicated habit
consuming distraction
tender with longing
pulling anger like a rope
that splits, frays, combusts

The mourning doves coo
into Sunday morning
how else do we habituate
the repetition follows the logic
of its own nascent order
frantic, curious, turbulent

I don't always mean what I say
the definition is shaded in questions

When sensation is too much for the body
we turn to our addictions, mine:

        stimulants / compulsive speech / discourse
        sedatives / a sea of silence / brooding

betrayal of the shadow, wailing animal
ecstatic, monstrous, erotic need

BEING PERCEIVED

You emerge from a known fact
heightened towards the other
for dramatic effect
our hearts broke off from the lush green
the folds of summer
under accusation, bitter fear

Scale down your power
you wanted to be flattered
as if a designation
could have an interior
your breathless confidence
you wept until you buckled
you were faking it worse than anyone

Le temps [. . .] n'est pas une forme d'intériorité, puisque c'est lui, au contraire, qui nous enveloppe. Loin que le temps nous soit intérieur, c'est nous qui habitons le temps.

Time . . . is not a form of interiority, since it is that which, on the contrary, envelops us. Far from being inside of us, it is we who inhabit time.

TIME

The vocabulary of her fear
undoes her femininity, in June
she weeps to exhaustion
zeroes out the heat of the
afternoon

Time is a pouring
it pools around the depression
settles in weakness, fatigue

Emotion exploits the body
splits the self at the instant
of process, defers integration
time is only ever lost
doubt is possessive
in certain moods, becomes
a temperament, a distraction

When every hormone produces a
declaration, just as easily
contradicted, each thought loops back
doubt eats it

She combs her hair
releases herself to the discourse
enables a hybridity
wanting nothing is a result
of being pushed to a brink
and held there
she pauses at the window
her hesitation hovers
feminine, loose, unwieldy

She is taken by a mysterious
shimmer in the trees
plastic trash in the sunlight
any sparkle becomes a thing of beauty
she is searching for a formal
representation of her thinking
the liminal hell of uncertainty
the murmur before a word

Without ever having dispelled
the shadow, time passes
around my body like an
atmosphere

The crickets still
chirping into dawn

I move into the weather
planes disrupting the blue
as much a part of the fabric
as anything

I float
with time's
passage
the way
something so
horrific
for a moment
then in time
a space
opens up
around the initial
piercing
of reality
apparent
safety

wherein
being participant is
allowing the terrible
passage
through silence
toward *a perception infinitely vaster*
being fallible, attached
within the matrix

TOTALITY

In the transparent daylight we were
slowly pivoting, like leaves
the motion was therapeutic, seasonal
undulation searching for a line
with terrible excitement that
suspends the course of time

We struggled to demonstrate the simple
truth of our affections
every agitation marked a boundary,
a threshold, a limit to the discrete
totality of a singular subject

Rustle of the leaves in the wind, frenetic
radio static through the kitchen window

the future is made up of this
contiguous present

the ineffable contemporary
stark and lush
vibrant and closed

We dream into time to let possibilities unravel . . .

       Lyrically, I'm loose as a thread, unspooled
       yet such hard tension resides just beneath
       the surface, ordinary bracing
       I wish to forget myself
       to blur, to fog, but the present
       is so precise: material as teeth

       .

La suspension n'est pas un temps arrêté avant qu'il se passe quelque chose, c'est l'événement même; l'entrée dans ce temps intime où en réalité la décision s'est déjà prise, mais nul ne le sait encore.

Suspension is not the arrested time that comes before something happens, it is the event itself; the passage into the intimate time where, in reality, the decision has already been made, but no one knows it yet.

IN SUSPENSE

Fields of distraction. The system is lost to chaos, so I attune to the naked blue of the winter sky.

This curse of impatience, this ordinary anxiety, cool minimum.

This stillness. Hum of airplanes like bees before the cold. Money shoved in envelopes and tucked into the drawer. Desire for an ending, an abiding fear: I absorb it. Make it my own while we wait. Suspend judgment. Prepare to leap without a pulse of muscle. You hang back, listen, choose to remain undetermined. The morning is long and I've lost track. I'm full of doubt. I'm flickering in fear.

Still thinking, sensing, interested with a wandering, absorptive awareness. I sigh into it, right here, the held breath; I can't stand it; don't want to; I turn in, unsettled. It's not intellectual. Sadness leaks into me. I'm a body of water.

In the morning's light I'm out
ahead of myself
I'm trembling at the shore
to keep the rush
that permanence betrays

Ripple in the cloud
ceiling of my thinking

Impatient is my mouth
yet I remain suspended
far from the weight
of any certainty
I float in doubt

This instant that bears no identity
between two shores, a fault
I'm seduced by the indeterminate
space of its event

I shut the door to claim this place
called my body, my breath
all caught up in my throat
the innocent drama of my longing

I trace a ring around my desire
it emanates a knowing light

artificial enclosure
the thick darkness of the
forest enters the periphery
of my dreams
passive imaginary:

> I'm climbing a stairwell
> metal exposure to the lightning storm at the
> shore, my knuckles wet
> my movements quick & determined

> Time passes like a bird
> all prior locutions being fallible
> in their sincerity
> past & future converge in the
> current of now
> the hour of meditation
> on the magic of the line
> cast out to the water

SHAME

Monday soft & still
shivering with cicadas

I'm obedient to the sound
silently I'm in attendance
to mystery as I clarify
the center of my devotion

Every day I'm alive again
debilitated by dread *gravity*
or light with desire *grace*

Being human in the pursuit of beauty
daily I must account for my errors, my regrets

Each of us has the capacity for cruelty
when desperate enough
threatened enough, afraid

I know mine well,
with the mind of the child, I do
identify with the worst of myself
I know better
I do it anyway

Experience reveals the intelligence of time
the passage of thought as sensation
I learn it over and over

I decide to shuck the excess
split from the day's accumulations
and swiftly ride to a place
not my own
to sit in the garden and admire
the intricate genius of flowers
walk to the wooded parts of the public park
to rest in the grass and shift my attention
between the singular, material details of the leaves
and the sky

*Être dépendant, c'est d'être
mal [. . .]. Et pourtant,
nous avons commencé là, dans
la dépendance la plus nue.
Violente [. . .]. Cet état
de dépendance première, nous
la cherchons et la fuyons
avec la même et constante
énergie.*

*To be dependent is to be
unwell . . . . And yet
we began there, in the most
naked dependency.
Violent . . . . This state
of primary dependency,
we seek it out and flee
from it with the same and
constant energy.*

DEPENDENCY

I rise from the bed, turn
and fall back again to
restless slumber,
dormant complicity with the night

I'm always catching the acts
of my betrayal,
departures from an initial &
ordinary intervention into time
I always return, but with faltering
focus

I let it be a little stupid, a little
treacherous, the hours
displace permanence while I
wait in attendance for a minute
of solitude, like a mother who
withdraws in advance of leaving

Night bends away from me
I wring out my dreams

The sky clears
the screen of my mind still
crowded with images
it shivers, fragmented & opaque
memory of a parallel elsewhere
devoid of choice
subject to the rupture of loss
a cruel disintegration
of coherence

The force of gravity
weighs upon me, the event
of his death can't float
indiscrete within the perimeter
of the pool, the morning

I bring a washcloth to my face & invoke your touch
brush the night's tangles from my hair & free my grip to you

I step out into the morning
I feel the cold on my face
I take pleasure in seeing my breath in the air
I multiply the matrix of my intimacies

Pink light in midwinter in the evening,
blush with the motion of need

Before dark you're under me like a shark in the glow,
freezing rain outside

I am up all night with the storm,
the changing landscape of the room
and the shape of us bending to the light

As the sun rises, I watch it cast
hot light among the branches
I treat light as an object
to set my gaze upon it
soothed by its inconstancy
how it softly shifts
across the wall

*Comment retourner
l'espoir sur le vif
du présent [. . .] ?*

*How to bend hope
toward the heart of
the present . . . ?*

HOPE NO MORE
near Leslie Scalapino's
"chameleon series"

Being unable to perceive
the situation
at the time
meaning first
to completely exit, being
devoid of the sting, seeing it
depersonalized
as fact, the shock which
cast me out
preferring to be reasonable

Meanwhile the dwelling pool of the
interior is full of history
mine, ours
the edge where the water meets
the earth, appearing, at first
fixed, solid, immutable
my pain, a known thing, and yet

Being not only past
what fresh water
is here, what
rainfall from a visiting
cloud brought on
by the winds
of change
of time
of circumstance

Let me be changed, then,
to transcend the limits of
perception already
known, the pool of fact
murky with weeds, slowly
in time, the waters will clear

When is   hope   a denial of the present reality, and when
a vital & generous force by which to grow?

Pink light of grace, the dawn
I move perpetually toward

NOT DYING

Face down in the blue. Beneath the surface is always another surface. Layers of opacity. A swimmer glides past, turns. The pool spills over, noiseless.

Soft, receding shape keeps hold from beyond. No guidance in this violet abyss, this blotted out gaze. Indisputable attachment: here, lining my body from the inside. It's cellular. How blue to linger parallel before you.   Not above, but the thin   transparent blue that's before, protecting the violet being singular   you   yes,   holding on,   the three of us   though you're apart   being blurred at the horizon.

Up close is the glow before the violet. I never waited, but return here often :   to the pool, feet wet in the memory. There is rest in the pitch purple. We are held in it, mute at the edge,   where you did sink but not now,   in the static stillness of the present hum.

I found words to pink at the crest, to make a wave to bring me back to you, eternal return. It's not painful except when the edge breaks like the dawn of our morning, swimming before breakfast.

Time displaces gravity. The rain turns to ice as it hits the ground. I am here below not with you. Unwilling humiliation drops into grief. I take refuge in the certain perimeter of the pool that keeps the memory static. It was over so quickly : bright breath of the morning. How cruel the memory of your final cries for help that echo in the halls of the foreign hotel. You were looking up, no final glance, no ending but the sound. I flip the record.

PART III

*La passion est la substance même
du risque. C'est ce reste de
passivité en nous qui s'affole au
contact de l'abrasion [. . .].
C'est notre capacité d'imaginer, de
s'étonner, d'être déçu, impressionné,
défait par quelque chose en nous
qui nous porte à aimer [. . .]
chaque détail de cet être qui bouge
devant nous, brève apparition de la
vie nue.*

*Passion is the very substance of risk.
It is this remainder of passivity
within that awakens on contact with an
abrasion . . . . It's our capacity to
imagine, to be astonished, disappointed,
impressed, undone by something within
ourselves that brings us to love . . .
every detail of this being who moves
before us, brief apparition of naked life.*

PASSION

Being wet is just one way of knowing. I want fresh, delicate spring in my mouth, a new rush, quick intellect independent of any fixed bond. When my center lights up I'm turned on. When my fingertips touch a petal's edge and the sky opens out. I notice new beauty when my neck is being kissed. When I feel my power, you're on your knees and the night is free. My body is fluent and whole. Your hair is wet and you're smiling.

Language leaves the body good, magenta stroke against the tide of logic makes my mouth water. Dip down in the current and lose your mind. It's alright. The edge is thin & sharp, it never breaks.

Come now, we're swimming. It's warm near the shore. It's raining. Touch the threat. It's pooling. It's not that dangerous, if you're willing. You've been here but not exactly. It's cooler now when your shoulders rise above the surface, toward the blue. We're between seasons. Time is a gully.

I'm disappearing into the rocks now, tide pools glinting with hidden life, treading water. There's always an ocean between us, joining us. It's primordial chaos, ecstatic thunder, a cosmic ring. You raise your arms and I'm aching to see you free.

What faint, cold thrill is this?

Being still inside this sensitive
expenditure—no measure for
what grants the material arrival
of language and at what pace

The figurative retreat is also
physical, foreseen, the changing weather

The bed is folded to the
wall, the curtain drawn
for night's confession
loss of the word until it's
spoken, another drop in the
pool   the heat between
enfolded palms that kept
a kiss

I keep my pleasures to myself now
neither demure nor insist
coiled & warm as a snake
I guard my focus
precious thing, necessary amid
the noise, doubt, diversion

I live with fear every day
and am not diminished for it

In my dark glasses, in the thin
air, again I pursue the sea
for whatever it is
I am after

Ce qu'on appelle infidélité est une forme d'exil hors de soi. *[. . .] Ce qui est vraiment inguérissable, c'est la fidélité.*

What is called infidelity is a form of exile outside of oneself. *. . . What is truly incurable is fidelity.*

MY FIDELITY IS MY OWN DISASTER
after Lisa Robertson

This, *my own disaster,* a violent
turn from any shared reality to the cold
exile of this private shell

What appears as choice is
undermined by a fearful hum,
a whole colony of bees
beneath the conscious surface
I live with the threat of their stings
numbly I go about the day's
rational decisions

*Buttoning the cuffs of my wrists and
the slit from my neck to my knees*

Nowhere am I more flawed, more fraught
with contradiction than in love

Point to my inconsistencies and I dissolve
become incomprehensible

The cool, hard surface of language creates a
medium of both protection and transmission that
acts between the energetic chaos (threatening
hum of my interior)
and the variable, shifting nature of relation

Within this discrete body
is an ocean of need

I live for the moments of grace when I can enter the
waves, stepping out from the shore at night, and the water
is welcoming, the violence of the waves crashes easily
against my body, the black sky meets the water's surface
at some invisible, distant horizon

I'm alone in the waves, I'm disappearing in shame, laughing, suffering in the break

I resent every moment when my pain thinks itself in isolation: imagines itself singular, exceptional, unusual

I long not to escape it, but for some refuge

> To be with you behind any closed door, let my head bow to the holy moment of approach, subdued by your measured force: reverent hands that touch with a knowledge of the depths of the quietest response, the subtlest murmur, a sigh

As I grieve I admire the light
without adjusting my body
simply looking out
in the August hum
sparrows flutter in and out of the frame

La rupture passe entre les êtres sans vraiment les altérer, elle les effleure, défait les liens, vient à bout de l'espérance passée, elle crée de nouvelles et inédites obligations, tout cela un peu en dehors de soi, comme si c'était finalement hors cadre.

A breakup passes between beings without really changing them; it wafts over them, undoes bonds, exhausts past hope, creates new and unanticipated obligations, all of it rather outside of oneself, as if, in the end, it happened out of bounds.

BREAKING UP

I was inside the choice to attend to the dreaded event, the gravity delayed. I got close to what was feared most to be a little less bracing about it. How humiliating, even in small doses, the apparent threat of loss. The reaction is animal, infantile, totally desperate.

I was looking for grace in the light of any imaginable circumstance, an unimaginable grief. I was asking for strength to allow this. I imagined and recollected at once, doubly landing in the present safety of the moment that allowed for the risk of imagining. I stayed in the apprehension of the light on the chair across the table, the breath that entered my lungs. Top teeth met the lower row and my elbows rested on the table just so.

I was collecting poppy seeds from breakfast on the tips of my fingers. Inconclusively my gaze drifted to rare sunshine through the front window. I was so afraid of losing. I bit down, took my vitamins.

REGRET

In the negative structure of
waiting I inhabit the hungry lack of a tourist
offer my need to the altar
of commerce
at the risk of regret, I take refuge
in a foreign solitude
the yes that ways a departure
from expectation

An afternoon in submission to the heat's gravity
tense with judgment, weary, despairing,
the sun brings me near to collapse

I stand beneath *The Ecstasy of Saint Teresa* as
she glows and discreetly snap a photo. She's awash in light
and I rearrange around my center, wavering in the heat,
irreverent, praying for grace to exceed the mind's narrowing.

Il est étrange de penser qu'aucune époque, peut-être, n'a été plus « sûre » que la nôtre, et pourtant nous souffrons tous d'une inquiétude grandissante, incommensurable à tout événement, à tout risque d'événement, devrais-je dire. [. . .] Le risque zéro, dans son énonciation, est une absurdité, puisque son effectivité annulerait la réalité même de ce dont il est question.

It's strange to think that perhaps no other era has been as "secure" as ours, and yet we all suffer from an increasing disquiet, incommensurable with any event, with any risk of an event, I should say. . . . The very concept of "zero risk" is absurd, for it, in effect, would annul the very reality to which it refers.

ZERO RISK

In the intellectual avoidance
of risk, which is the attempt
to be in control, the chance at
wonder is compromised

What's new already here
in the reality perceptible to the mind's eye
of the inner child, fresh with awe
uninhibited delight

I take refuge in details, soft curl of a petal
pinks the edge of my discomfort
this singular colour is a certain, vibrant glow

PART IV

Is it urgent to bring to consciousness one's darkest thoughts, silently, secretly, in cool air, through the streets?

—Etel Adnan

SPEECH

With a prayer, I step from the plane
and into the conviction of my irrational decision

I release the fist of regret, and swiftly
I'm with the propulsive energy of desire

I've marked your skin where you left me wordless
replenished by the soft intensity of your attention
the weight of your gaze

I'm touched by the indelible image
of the blue ceiling
the grace of your restraint
my fear dissolved into chosen surrender, the pressure
of my teeth on your neck

When we speak, when we touch, when we sit
silent and alert on the train, attuned
the space between us a tunnel, the phenomenal
world a stream of passing noise & colour

In time I will tell you what I couldn't speak
in submission to the current of sensation,
the depths of the water, indigo of evening
as I willed my legs to obey, to fall into step
at your side, stunned by your beauty

I'm not yours but you have me
wet at the elevator doors until they close
to eclipse your face,
the presence of your touch still hot in me

Morning, heat breaks to an August storm
and I'm drinking back the water I gave to kissing you for hours,
save for the brief benediction of sleep

SPEECH (REPRISE)

Whip that cuts the silence
offers no resolve
eternal torment
the condition
we name & graze infinity
insight being just another
sensation

We're here to understand what we already know:
here, separating time to distinguish a presence,
here, in the chaotic, simultaneous, primordial perfection

With a word, we enter the break
disclose some clues
to our perceptions, vast interior
meeting point between material
illusion and the universal sea

Still we speak, as *rivers do meet, waters submit themselves to the ocean's attraction*

Sincere & flawed
this speech betrays my
knowing, exposes false speculation
and, like a teacher, strikes me
into humility

Who knew I was waiting all this time
for you?

NOT KNOWING

To be in the fog is to be in a state of suspension. What's true is then not true.

What is at risk in the event of suspense, the cool light of dawn, heat just below the horizon. Dreams drop you into the untenable posture of what's about to be: the silence preceding the action still undetermined, already decided. Being at the center of apprehension, the void and its apparent emptiness, still clutching to the rock.

I'm overcome with longing for the mountains: the elemental understanding of belonging to a place. I'm limp beneath an indeterminate light. Fatigue displaces stillness as the mind drifts. Trembling in mystery, weak with inhibition, I faint into the sentence.

Wild with impatience but so slow. I'm struck down by obscurity, unable to move, fog passes irreducibly across my thinking. Why then this faltering uncertainty, timid mistrust of the order of things. It's not a crisis, this permanent emptiness, pure, unbroken whole.

Cette disposition à la déception est, paradoxalement, une réserve intacte d'imaginaire [. . .] qui lui permet d'apprivoiser le réel et d'y loger, comme un dispositif secret, son horizon d'attente.

This liability to disappointment is, paradoxically, an intact reserve of the imaginary . . . which makes it possible for one to tame the real & to lodge oneself in it, like a secret apparatus, one's horizon of expectation.

FAILURE

Failure became a form of
possibility, there, shimmering
at the fallen horizon, so slight:
the hour was incumbent
upon us, we listened for the
hum & roar as the autumn
roses opened their buds
deep red reaching, flush
of peach in September, full
of luster that turns interior,
floral delirium

The day's fresh sunlight
draws me toward it, easily
I brighten, take flight
curved & reflective
pliant & wise
for the season

FACILITY

I step into the shower to free
the run-off of my thinking
about the feeling: by nature
preceding the word

I meet a desire to betray
my own sincerity, at the foot
of the bed, the empty glass
of my confusion

Life is too close. I need
a forest, a little stream
to walk alongside,
instead, the city advances
toward me

The day is made up
of digressions:
I sigh, I drift, still
expectant, cautious
streams of thought
filter through my body

I'm at the surface now, as the clouds thin
I'm looking up

PART V

Dès qu'on a un point d'éternité dans l'âme, on n'a rien de plus à faire que de le préserver, car il s'accroit de lui-même, comme une graine.

—Simone Weil

As soon as there is a point of eternity in the soul, there is nothing more to do than to preserve it, for it will grow of itself like a seed.

SWEET DESCENT

I'm speaking now as if to you alone,
and the ground has a sweeter scent
I'm quick and knowing as a snake
end to end, heat to cool along the earth

I know what it is to drop into the truth
of the seed: I descend, touch the
arterial intelligence of the root system
and am brought to guidance, this soft
steady hum

The system that is my body harmonizes,
always available to the primordial sound
unfettered, my devotion runs deep

You held me there where the ache resides
split of the heart, pelvic hunger
for erotic sustenance
a grief that traverses the
inner channel to settle in the jaw
unexpressed sound

I sigh in the memory of your palms
shudder as I close my eyes, and the
sound travels through me, into me, even now
I'm fed by you

Si je marche au flanc d'une montagne, je peux voir d'abord un lac, puis, après quelques pas, une forêt. Il faut choisir : ou le lac ou la forêt. Si je veux voir à la fois le lac et la forêt, je dois monter plus haut.

Seulement la montagne n'existe pas. Elle est faite d'air. On ne peut pas monter : il faut être tiré.

—Simone Weil, "Contradiction"

If I walk along a mountainside, I can see first a lake, then, after a few steps, a forest. It is necessary to choose : the lake or the forest. If I want to see both the lake and the forest at once, I must climb higher.

Except the mountain does not exist : it is made of air. We cannot climb, we must be drawn up.

A COLD, DARK LAKE

In both prayer & poem, this act of attention which
moves from the body toward the sky. This desire for
perfection, not to be forgiven by any singular god,
but to remember an inherent coherence with the law of
beauty   nature's perfection

What wicked corruption would suggest the effort
perpetually insufficient. With neither teacher nor discipline,
innocent heads turn toward the sun, the way we recognize
god in one another so easily, the light in your eyes the
moment we met.

In a city swarming with potential encounters I am
forever possessed by impossible questions of providence:
what brings us toward one another, what force, what
intelligence, what outside the ordinary, functional realm of
the visible.

Impatient with the ordinary I want only to meet the sacred
in you, and I want it fast

then patient forever in the unfolding, as if we had
lifetimes to know each other, as if we have already done
this, in other bodies.

I rush to you & wait: time passes   things align
when   force   is removed

I am lit up by desire, fervent to feel you
palm to palm, and *let lips do what hands do;*
    they pray, grant thou,
    lest faith turn to despair

To be held against a wall & let my body learn to release
to you

I live for this indeterminate edge:
not endurance, it's more sensitive than that

To stay with the signal of resistance
let my body breathe into the threshold

To receive you takes time,
a soft focus makes my chest light
the noise outside dims with the curtain drawn

Lush in the forest, I'm lit up with your tongue
on the curve of my ear, the length
of my neck that extends to you

I relax my jaw

I want to lose my mind
to ride the lip of control
until you make me gasp

I resist what I want: to succumb to you,
to the pleasure, the supple pressure
of your dominance, the thrill of your
restraint

Under your thumb, I begin to perceive
my capacity to submit
to want little   &   feel deeply

What a gift to be slowed
down, close
to death
to dreaming
it's subliminal
ecstatic
deep
pool
of blue
a cold, dark lake

imperceptible floor

CONTRADICTION

Alive to the sensational pulse of opposition,
the day is replete with choice, surfaces of possibility

I bend to the rose that blooms amid the noise

Within any heady, aromatic bliss is a seed of desolation
the task is to include it all

A training of the spirit that orients toward the good
beauty without denial of evil   *corruption*

I worship contradiction to know we are not doomed
wickedness like horses behind the stranger's eyes

I run headlong toward the light knowing the darkness is
with me

FAITH

Elsewhere the possibility horizon of another way to feel glows
Steadily I set my regard upon it,   across the distance
between this cold, contracted pain   and what's there

Supple in the extension between what I am   & what I love:
    a lightness, a conviction, a warm, angelic flush

    I'm diving into the waves, totally free,
    detached, absorbed: this is how I know
    surrender

I'm staying in fear's shell
to cup the private spiral

    I long to be buoyed by faith
    it has a strength all its own
    equal to my terror

The information of my fear
is generous, delicate, pours through me

I refuse to rely on the muscular strength of the will

Something bright & quiet in me is changing
how can I tell the you that is also, always an I

This pain is never mine alone, yet I treat it how I want to
  Under these conditions, betrayal is impossible
I can be both afraid & joyous at once:
  a glimmer of happiness for what might elsewhere destroy me
As I realize my choice, my power
  I'm not wrecked by my emotions when I respect their intelligence
I create a gap between humiliation & desire
  I float in the interval

VOID

Gone the impulse for escape so I might return, drop back
to the centreline & be satisfied. Fresh is the day's light and
its multiplicities.

Repeatedly I am presented with apparent limits to my
perception, closed ground, facts collapse beneath my gaze.
Latent defiance to the noise, lurid assault on the senses.
I cool my patience in the waiting room, the quality of my
thought diminished to what's necessary. Shutter the blinds,
I'm horizontal.

I cross the intersection like a ghost, blinking. The beauty
of the weather is lost on me.

Time is spacious, sunlit. I carry your questions like bread.
I'm outside of thought, flush with the artifice of the
city, brutal containment. I contract, conserve, drop down
beneath the hum, the clamour on the edge of need,
secretive want that pulses beneath the functional rhythm
of the day.

Il faut se prêter à autrui et ne se donner qu'à soi-même.

—Michel de Montaigne

Elsewhere I fling myself into
the day with unabashed desire
It wears me out
I return to the refuge of
my solitude, tend the source
in the measure of what to keep
& what to give away

as if to learn the stakes
of indulgence, the cost
of restraint

> *You must lend yourself to others
> and give yourself only to yourself.*

Reculer devant l'objet qu'on poursuit. Seul ce qui est indirect est efficace. On ne fait rien si l'on n'a d'abord reculé. En tirant sur la grappe, on fait tomber les grains à terre.

—Simone Weil

To draw back before the object of one's pursuit. Only that which is indirect is effective. We do nothing if we have not first drawn back. To pull at the branch makes all the grapes fall to the ground.

LONGING

In the texture of longing
intimate wait I concentrate
on the distance between
what I am and what I desire
an irreconcilable set of imperatives

Several frames flash before me
and I do not turn away
but remain to face the
insecurity of multiplicity
it can't be regulated

Repeatedly I pull back
from the descendent force
of melancholy,
its dwelling pool

to rather hover on the surface
of chance,   sense the ripple
as the wind changes direction

MORTAL PROVIDENCE

Impossible to realize this task of decreation
still the I hungers to be emptied
being human
worn out by a riot of nightmares
jade morning
the cool rustling of dawn
calls me forth
to remove the splinter of night
hot infection

What kind of attention
is deprived of need
I'm so full of desire
reverent vitality

There's no question of letting go, now
releasing my throat from your grip
vibrant as a stream in the sun
I swallow to tend this light in me

ENDNOTES: ON THE COMMUNAL
NECESSITY OF WRITING

I feel like all the work is collaborative work, it's just that it comes out under an individual name so the other people you're in collaboration with are subordinated . . . to [your] own name, even though all of those voices are constantly with you and in your head.
            —Fred Moten

I am thankful to Sara Jane Stoner, who introduced me to the writing of Anne Dufourmantelle, and whose friendship and editorial guidance have been absolutely vital to the spirit of this book. I am thankful to Venn Daniel, who physically handed me a copy of *In Praise of Risk* to read. The beginning of this project, and my choice to take the risk to begin, was nurtured by the faith and conspiring friendship of Asiya Wadud. I am thankful to the Poetry Project, whose Emerge-Surface-Be fellowship supported the initial stages of this book. The Poetry Project also published an earlier version of the poem "Suspense" in their journal, *The Recluse*.

The successive wave of momentum that carried this book to completion came forth through my meeting and being with Lee Bullit, whose presence streams through many of these poems. Living in the dailiness of writing and translation has been sustained through exchanges, both direct and psychic, with Hoda Adra, imogen xtian smith, Phoebe Fregoli, Adriana Disman, Sarah Riggs, Sasha J. Langford, Benjamin Krusling, and Morgan Võ: thank you each. I am thankful to Cub for an enduring belief in my writing, and celebration of every phase of the process. I am thankful to Karishma Kripalani who held space for the inner spectres of doubt which inhibited this book's actualization. I am thankful to Rupali for covering the sushi bill. I am thankful to adjacent writing and thinking with Anna Moschovakis, whose mentorship is with me always, and whose study of Dufourmantelle inspired her own writing on the subject of risk. I am thankful to Nathanaël, whose light of attention illumined sites of creative possibility within the mutable process of translation.

Finally, I am thankful to the collective vision and devoted labour of everyone at Wendy's Subway—and particularly to Corinne Butta and Rachel Valinsky for conversations on the subway and in the reading room—for their careful attention and commitment to seeing this book through.

Excerpts from Anne Dufourmantelle throughout the collection are italicized in blue. Translations are at times my own, at times that of the published translator, Steven Miller, from *In Praise of Risk* (New York: Fordham University Press, 2019), and at others a weaving of the two. The following are page and chapter citations for passages from Dufourmantelle's original *Éloge du risque* (Paris: Payot & Rivages, 2011).

p. 12: « *Désir, corps, écriture* », p. 204.

p. 16: « *Au risque de la beauté* », pp. 242, 244.

p. 18: Ibid., p. 244.

p. 22: « *D'une perception infiniment plus vaste [. . .]* », pp. 97–98.

p. 24: « *Au risque de l'éblouissement* », p. 201.

p. 28: « *La prophétie intime* », pp. 188–189.

p. 38: « *Assiduité* », p. 234.

p. 44: « *Ce temps qu'on dit perdu* », p. 88.

p. 52: « *En suspens* », p. 29.

p. 60: « *Minuscules magiques dépendances* », pp. 21–22.

p. 66: « *Ne plus espérer* », p. 162.

p. 74: « *Au risque de la passion* », p. 36.

p. 80: « *Inguérissables (in)fidélités* », pp. 58, 60.

p. 86: « *Rompre* », p. 130.

p. 90: « *Risque zéro?* », pp. 62–63.

p. 100: « *L'adieu au monde magique. Par-delà la déception* », p. 110.

A CATALOGUE OF RISK

INTRODUCTION
p. 5: Fanny Howe, *Night Philosophy* (Brussels: Divided Publishing, 2020).

p. 13: Lucille Clifton, ". . . why / is there under that poem always / an other poem?" in *Black Nature: Four Centuries of African American Nature Poetry*, ed. Camille T. Dungy (Athens, GA: University of Georgia Press, 2009).

PART I
p. 23: Fanny Howe, *Night Philosophy*.

p. 25: Benjamin Krusling, *Glaring* (Brooklyn, NY: Wendy's Subway, 2020).

p. 29: Laura Henriksen, in conversation (2022).

PART II
p. 34: *The Kena Upanishad* is a Vedic text classified as one of the *Mukhya Upanishads* and estimated to have been originally written down around the middle of the first millennium BCE. Eknath Easwaran, *The Upanishads* (Tomales, CA: Nilgiri Press, 1987).

p. 67: Leslie Scalapino, *That They Were at the Beach: Aeolotropic Series* (San Francisco: North Point Press, 1985).

p. 68: Zen Buddhist concept, "Muddy water is best cleared by leaving it alone." Alan Watts, *The Way of Zen* (New York: Vintage Books, 1989).

p. 71: Carm Mascarenhas, *Someday Soon*, Mascanta Music, 1975, LP.

PART III
p. 76: Act 4, Scene 3 in William Shakespeare, *Romeo and Juliet* (New York: Simon & Schuster, 2004).

p. 81: Lisa Robertson, *Lisa Robertson's Magenta Soul Whip* (Toronto, CA: Coach House Books, 2005).

p. 81: Sylvia Plath, *Ariel* (New York: Faber & Faber, 2010).

p. 82: Sara Jane Stoner, in conversation (2021).

PART IV
p. 94, 98: Etel Adnan, *There: In the Light and the Darkness of the Self and of the Other* (New York: The Post-Apollo Press, 1997).

p. 99: Etel Adnan, *Sea and Fog* (New York: Nightboat Books, 2012).

PART V
pp. 106, 110: Simone Weil, "*L'Attention et la volonté,*" in *La pesanteur et la grâce* (Paris: République des Lettres, 2019).

p. 112: Act 1, Scene 5 in Shakespeare, *Romeo and Juliet*.

p. 114: Addi Kamb, in conversation (2022).

p. 120: Michel de Montaigne in *Vivre sa vie*, directed by Jean-Luc Godard (1962; Les Films de la Pléiade, Pathé Consortium Cinéma).

p. 122: Simone Weil, "*L'Attention et la volonté.*"

p. 123: Lisa Robertson, *Lisa Robertson's Magenta Soul Whip* (Toronto, CA: Coach House Books, 2005).

ENDNOTES
p. 129: Fred Moten, "An Interview with Fred Moten, Part One," interview with Adam Fitzgerald, *Lit Hub,* 2015.

A Catalogue of Risk
© 2025 Alisha Mascarenhas

All rights reserved. No part of this book may be used or reproduced without prior permission of the publisher.

Passage Series #7
First Edition, 2025
Edition of 1,000 copies
ISBN 979-8-9909878-1-4
LCCN 2024940957

Edited by Corinne Butta
Proofread by Rachel Valinsky
Designed by Dorothy Lin
Typeset in Times LT
   and Tempos Mono
Printed at Tallina
   Raamatutrükikoda, Estonia

Published by Wendy's Subway
379 Bushwick Avenue
Brooklyn, NY 11206
wendyssubway.com

Wendy's Subway is a non-profit reading room, writing space, and independent publisher located in Brooklyn.

The Passage Series features titles by emerging writers and artists whose work manifests in innovative, hybrid, and cross-genre forms that imagine new possibilities and expressions of the poetic, the political, and the social.

A Catalogue of Risk was selected as the 2022 Carolyn Bush Award recipient.

The Passage Series is supported, in part, by the New York State Council on the Arts with support of the Office of the Governor and the New York State Legislature; public funds from the New York City Department of Cultural Affairs in Partnership with the City Council; and the Robert Rauschenberg Foundation.